MW00744952

INTRODUCTION

Each day in the *ONE Student Journal*, you will explore scripture using seven key words. The content following the words is designed to help you understand the concepts of the passage and make personal application.

The seven words are:

1. **THINK**
2. **READ**
3. **DISCOVER**
4. **EXPERIENCE**
5. **CONSIDER**
6. **PRAY**
7. **JOURNAL**

① THINK

Everybody likes a good story, right? Each day your *ONE Journal* begins with a story to help you grasp the meaning of the daily passage.

② READ

The purpose of the *ONE Journal* is to provide a tool for personal time in God's Word. Read the entire passage of scripture. However, note there will always be a couple of verses which are highlighted with these words *"Focus on…"* These are key verses, so give them a little extra attention.

③ DISCOVER

Every day, you'll discover the answer to this question: *"What does the scripture teach in this passage?"* The space where you write begins with a few words to help in your discovery.

④ EXPERIENCE

The Bible was never meant to be simply read, memorized and quoted. It was meant to be experienced! This section is about making personal application of what you read. Ask yourself this question: *"What does the passage mean to me in my life?"* Every day think about the verses in relationship to your real life experiences.

⑤ CONSIDER

There are some days when you read a passage and do not have a clue what it means. The consider section is a group of questions which may be used in two ways. First, to help understand the passage on those tough days. Second, if you want to dig a little deeper into the passage and find more, the questions can serve to challenge your thinking!

⑥ PRAY

Make prayer a part of your day. The *ONE Journal* provides a place each day for you to list your prayer concerns. Perhaps they are about friends, family members or yourself (even that upcoming test!). Just write them down using this section.

⑦ JOURNAL

Journaling is important for everyone, so we have provided a little space for you to write those things that are on your mind or heart. Sometimes we have things we are thinking about that we just need to put into writing. So go ahead, use this journal to make journaling a habit.

Encourage a friend to join you on this journey! Having a friend as an accountability partner will help keep you on track during those difficult days. Sharing what God is teaching you each day through His Word is a great way to make the truth of the Bible become real in your life. If both of you are doing the same journal, then sharing is even more effective.

THINK

Injustice is a part of life in the world around us. The daily news on your phone or computer shows children who are hungry or mistreated. You probably know someone in your school or sphere of influence who is a victim. In spite of this type of treatment, these same people often demonstrate gracious, forgiving spirits.

Walt was one of those people. He was a student in a Christian school who desired to serve the Lord. However, instead of being encouraged or honored, Walt was ridiculed.

You see, Walt was different. He had MS (Multiple Sclerosis), so it was difficult for him to walk or use his hands. When he spoke, his speech was slurred, and it took him a long time to say what he wanted to say.

Others mocked and mimicked him. On more than one occasion he cried, but he never got angry. When asked why he didn't get angry, Walt smiled and said, "They don't know any better, so I choose to forgive them!"

Walt had adopted the same mindset that Jesus demonstrates in our passage for today. Forgiveness is a choice!

READ

LUKE 23:26-38

Focus on ...

"When they came to the place called the Skull, they crucified him there, along with the criminals—one on his right, the other on his left. Jesus said, 'Father, forgive them, for they do not know what they are doing'" (vv. 33-34a)

DISCOVER

The basic truth is:

EXPERIENCE

As a result I will:

CONSIDER

- Why didn't Jesus fight those who crucified him?
- Think about the sensitivity of Jesus to others even on the cross.
- Why did Jesus forgive his enemies?
- Notice the response of the people to Jesus' forgiveness.

PRAY

In response to this passage, I will pray for:

JOURNAL

I just have to write about:

THINK

"I have already beaten you up once, and I will do it again if you keep talking about Jesus!"

Mike could not believe Larry had come back a second time to talk to him about Jesus. Just two weeks earlier, Mike had beaten Larry up and sent him home. Now he was back again.

It was Larry's words this time that really got Mike's attention. Larry told Mike he had forgiven him. Then he said something that changed Mike's life forever: "I know you can beat me up, but this is important, so I am going to tell you anyway."

Larry not only had the compassion to forgive Mike, he also had the courage to approach him again with the gospel. It was both Larry's forgiveness and courage that made Mike listen the second time.

Why was Larry willing to forgive Mike? Why was he willing to risk being hurt again? He was compelled by the love of Christ, just as Stephen was in the passage we read today.

READ

ACTS 7:54-60

Focus on ...

"Then he fell on his knees and cried out, 'Lord, do not hold this sin against them.' When he had said this, he fell asleep" (v 60).

DISCOVER

The basic truth is:

_____

_____

_____

_____

EXPERIENCE

As a result I will:

_____

_____

_____

_____

_____

_____

CONSIDER

- Stephen was a deacon, not a pastor.
- Stephen knew he was preaching an unpopular message.
- Why would Stephen choose to forgive his enemies?
- Do you think Stephen was influenced by Jesus' example to forgive?

PRAY

In response to this passage, I will pray for:

_____

_____

_____

_____

_____

JOURNAL

I just have to write about:

_____

_____

_____

_____

_____

_____

_____

_____

_____

_____

_____

_____

_____

THINK

Zach told the truth. Honesty should be rewarded, right? Obviously, not everyone in the class agreed on that point. Especially since it meant the teacher would not be grading on a curve.

"Come on, Zach! Don't be so righteous." "Who do you think you are, anyway—the Pope?" These were just a couple of the comments Zach was pelted with as he made his decision. He had discovered the answer key to the exam had been posted on the Internet, and he felt reporting it was the right thing to do.

To say he took some flack would be an understatement. He was downright persecuted, even by some of the students he thought had integrity. Even one faculty member took a verbal shot at him, sending the classroom into a roar of laughter.

Zach knew he had done the right thing, so he quietly took the verbal barbs that came his way. He had decided his character was worth the pain. He had also decided not to get angry, but to patiently endure the consequences.

Just like in our passage today, Zach chose to suffer patiently. Although some of his friends made fun of him, he did the right thing—as far as God was concerned.

READ

1 PETER 2:19-21

Focus on...
"But how is it to your credit if you receive a beating for doing wrong and endure it? But if you suffer for doing good and you endure it, this is commendable before God" (v.20).

DISCOVER

The basic truth is:

EXPERIENCE

As a result I will:

PRAY

In response to this passage, I will pray for:

JOURNAL

I just have to write about:

THINK

Tony sat on the bench, never really expecting to get in the game. All of that changed when he heard the assistant coach call, "Tony, get your gear. You're up!" For a moment he sat there stunned, until the coach yelled his name again.

Tony was a member of the team: he had a uniform, he practiced with the team and he knew all the plays. However, if he had never answered the coach's call to get off the bench and get in the game, he would have been nothing more than a spectator with a good seat.

The prophet Isaiah had a similar story. He was a man of God who was ready to serve and responded when God called his number. His response proved his openness to whatever God had for his life. He was willing to go anywhere and do anything for the Lord.

There are a lot of Christians on the team. They wear the uniform, come to practice each week at church and know all the plays (Bible verses). Yet some of them continue to sit on the bench, even when God is calling them to get into the game. They are content to just have a good seat.

READ

ISAIAH 6:1-8

Focus on ...

"Then I heard the voice of the Lord saying, 'Whom shall I send? And who will go for us?' And I said, 'Here am I. Send me!'" (v. 8)

DISCOVER

The basic truth is:

_____

_____

_____

_____

EXPERIENCE

As a result I will:

_____

_____

_____

_____

_____

_____

CONSIDER

- What was Isaiah's attitude when he was called into the game?
- Spectator Christianity is not enough ... we need participants!
- Are you in the game or just occupying a good seat?
- How can you be more open to God's leading in your life?

PRAY

In response to this passage, I will pray for:

_____

_____

_____

_____

_____

JOURNAL

I just have to write about:

_____

_____

_____

_____

_____

_____

_____

_____

_____

_____

_____

_____

_____

THINK

He was an unlikely leader. When the call to leadership came, he was not doing anything that set him apart. When he was approached about the position, at first he hid, and then he protested with excuses about family.

He continued to fight against the idea, even when he realized it was already decided. If most men had been offered the position by this authority, they would have felt honored and jumped at the chance. But not Gideon. He was afraid.

Perhaps you remember the story of Gideon in Judges 6 and his reluctance to accept God's invitation to leadership. Yes, he was outnumbered, and yes, the plan *did* seem impractical. However, God had never lost a battle, and He could be trusted. The question was: would Gideon step up to the plate?

In the *Woodlawn* movie, Tony had to answer the same question that you do—the question of trusting and obeying God. Just as He had a plan for Tony's life, He has one for yours, as well.

You may feel insignificant or inadequate for the task, but God can do great things through you. Do not worry about your abilities, just make yourself *available* to God's plan.

READ

Focus on ...

"So they inquired further of the Lord, 'Has the man come here yet?' And the Lord said, 'Yes, he has hidden himself among the supplies.' They ran and brought him out, and as he stood among the people he was a head taller than any of the others" (vv. 22-23).

DISCOVER

The basic truth is:

EXPERIENCE

As a result I will:

CONSIDER

- What was Gideon doing when he was called to leadership?
- Gideon's response was just like that of many people: he questioned God.
- Do you have to agree with God's plan to accept it and obey?
- Are you willing to step out for God against the odds?

PRAY

In response to this passage, I will pray for:

JOURNAL

I just have to write about:

THINK

You have just been voted the class president. Your coach told the team you are the best player and made you team captain. You made the honor roll again, and the principal asked for your advice about how to improve the school's environment.

OK, this sounds too good to be true. You are thinking this would not even happen in your dreams. But for just a moment, let's pretend it *is* true. How do you think you would respond? Perhaps the better question is how *should* you respond?

Admittedly it would be tough to stay humble if all of these things were happening at the same time. However, if you stop and consider why you were given your talents and abilities, it might not be that difficult. See, according to the Scriptures, those who are the greatest (most gifted) are to be the servants of others.

The abilities you possess were given to you by God. He places you in positions so you can be salt and light and serve others. He also reminds us that if we do not humble ourselves, we may be humbled by others or even by Him. Humility is a difficult concept because you cannot fake it. You either have the right attitude and it is demonstrated through humility, or you don't, and it's not!

Jesus clearly explains the role of the servant leader. He talks about a person with great ability who maintains humility. The person Jesus is describing is not a "lowly" person but a "great" person. However, they do not dwell on their greatness because they tend to focus on others.

READ

MATTHEW 23:1-12

Focus on ...

"The greatest among you will be your servant. For those who exalt themselves will be humbled, and those who humble themselves will be exalted" (vv. 11-12).

DISCOVER

The basic truth is:

EXPERIENCE

As a result I will:

CONSIDER

- Humility is an attitude that lives out in an action.
- How do you respond when you succeed at something?
- True humility treats people with dignity.
- Do you want to be a leader if leading means serving?

PRAY

In response to this passage, I will pray for:

JOURNAL

I just have to write about:

THINK

Running wind sprints was Ryan's least favorite part of football practice. He could not see any benefit in the exercise as it related to his position. He was an offensive linemen and did not plan on doing much running. But his coach was not the kind of man you complained to about his coaching.

Day after day, week after week, Ryan practiced blocking but also ran and ran. Each day, he noticed he was not as out of breath as he had been on the preceding days. He still did not like running, but he obviously was building up his endurance.

Finally, the first game of the season arrived, and Ryan was ready to play ball. He hit the field, never realizing he would end up playing almost two thirds of the game. As the time moved on, he became keenly aware of the reason for the wind sprints.

The other team's defense was dragging around the field, out of shape and out of breath, but *he* felt great. The so called "mundane" training he had endured during practice had given him and his team a distinct advantage. They were a strong fourth quarter team.

So it was with David, the giant killer. Because he was faithful in the "mundane" thing of tending sheep, he was ready for battle. While tending the sheep, he had defended them against a lion and bear. What incredible practice for giant killing.

READ

Focus on ...

"'The Lord who rescued me from the paw of the lion and the paw of the bear will rescue me from the hand of this Philistine.'
Saul said to David, 'Go, and the Lord be with you'" (v. 37).

DISCOVER

The basic truth is:

_____

_____

_____

_____

_____

EXPERIENCE

As a result I will:

_____

_____

_____

_____

_____

_____

CONSIDER

- The mundane requirements of life usually precede great moments.
- Ryan did not get the "big picture" until he was in the real game.
- Was David bragging on *himself* or *God* when he talked about the lion and bear?
- What mundane thing do you dislike that is necessary for preparation?

PRAY

In response to this passage, I will pray for:

JOURNAL

I just have to write about:

THINK

Have you ever read the children's classic book *The Adventures of Pinocchio*? It is one of the most well-read pieces of children's literature ever. It has inspired hundreds of editions, stage plays and movies, such as Walt Disney's iconic animated version.

Pinocchio was created out of wood by a wood carver named *Geppetto*. Although loved and cared for, Pinocchio wanted more: he wanted to be like the other boys. He decided he would venture out on his own.

Pinocchio wanted what he wanted, he had his own plans, and *Geppetto* did not matter. If you remember, in the cartoon version, he got into trouble, was swallowed by a whale and was hopelessly doomed. All of this came about because he was not willing to fulfill the plan of his creator.

You and I are not so different. According to our passage today, we have been created by God "unto good works." He has a plan for our lives, but often we want what we want. Therefore, we abandon the safety of being in His care and go out to follow our own personal desires.

READ

EPHESIANS 2:4-10

Focus on ...

"For we are God's handiwork, created in Christ Jesus to do good works, which God prepared in advance for us to do" (v. 10).

DISCOVER

The basic truth is:

EXPERIENCE

As a result I will:

CONSIDER

- God created you for a purpose. Do you know what it is?
- God did not create you to be a puppet like Pinocchio.
- You have free will and can make choices about your life!
- Are you content to be in God's care and His will?

PRAY

In response to this passage, I will pray for:

_____

_____

_____

_____

_____

JOURNAL

I just have to write about:

_____

_____

_____

_____

_____

_____

_____

_____

_____

_____

_____

_____

THINK

The revolving doors in New York City buildings are intriguing. They are in hotels and businesses up and down every street, and they are *huge*!

A little boy who was about 5 years old, was inside one of those buildings. He eyed the revolving door and wanted to play in it, so he kept pulling on his mother's hand. Time and again he pulled, but she was resolute in holding him firmly, each time telling him no. Finally he sprang free and bolted into the doors. His mother made no attempt to rescue him.

He began going around and around, each time celebrating his independence. After the fourth time around he was ready to exit, but didn't know how, so he began to cry. The wise mother never moved. She just watched him circle a couple more times to make her point, knowing he was in no danger.

Then, by sticking her arm inside at just the right, the automatic eye stopped the door's motion, and the little boy was freed. His mother gently wrapped her arms around him, but firmly chastised him.

The psalmist reminds us that the wisest and safest place to be is waiting on the Lord. Being with *Him* gives us courage and makes our hearts strong. Unfortunately, we tend to have the same problem as the 5 year old: we want to pull away to show our independence.

READ

PSALM 27:11-14

Focus on...
"Wait for the LORD;
be strong and take heart
and wait for the LORD" (v. 14).

DISCOVER

The basic truth is:

EXPERIENCE

As a result I will:

CONSIDER

- The safest place for any believer is close to the Lord.
- One of our greatest struggles is the desire for independence!
- Are you fearful about facing life? Could it be you have pulled away?
- What do you think it means to "wait" on the Lord?

PRAY

In response to this passage, I will pray for:

JOURNAL

I just have to write about:

THINK

According to Voice of the Martyrs website, Sudanese Christians face poverty, war and genocide. Christian villages face daily bombings by the Sudanese military as they try to eradicate black Sudanese in the Nuba Mountains. They are trying to eliminate all Christian villages, churches, hospitals and schools in an effort to Islamize the country. The National Intelligence Security Services (NISS) has raided, occupied or bulldozed churches and continues to arrest and deport Nubians and South Sudanese.

One Christian lady who was killed because she would not run was Neima Abiad Idris. Though her songs are not likely to be heard on your local Christian radio station, the music of this talented Christian woman was well known in Sudan's Nuba Mountains.

Neima, 49, was a wife and mother of six whose life was cut short by bomb shrapnel on Nov. 6, 2014 when an Antonov bomb struck her home village of Kadir in the Nuba Mountains. Neima's life testimony represents the faith and courage of so many Nubian Christians.

Neima, like the apostles in our passage today, believed they should obey God rather than man. Neima paid the price with her life. The apostles were beaten for their faith. You will probably never face physical persecution, but you might get a little flack about your faith. Somehow that just doesn't seem significant in light of the price some people pay.

READ

ACTS 5:27-32

Focus on ...

"Peter and the other apostles replied: 'We must obey God rather than human beings!'" (v. 29)

DISCOVER

The basic truth is:

EXPERIENCE

As a result I will:

CONSIDER

- You probably will never face physical persecution, but what if ... ?
- Taking a stand for Jesus takes courage, conviction and commitment!
- What is the hardest thing you have ever suffered for your faith?
- The apostles were not being difficult—they were just honoring God.

PRAY

In response to this passage, I will pray for:

_____

_____

_____

_____

JOURNAL

I just have to write about:

_____

_____

_____

_____

_____

_____

THINK

Tara knew her Christianity was pretty much in name only. She really did not live out her faith. Then came the weekend retreat with her church, and on the very first night, her heart was stirred. The meeting ended, and she was in tears, knowing what she needed to do.

She approached Rebecca, one of the leaders, and asked for her help. Rebecca had reached out to her on several occasions, but Tara had rejected her efforts, assuring the leader that she was OK spiritually. Now Tara confessed what Rebecca already suspected: her life was a mess!

Over the next few months, the two of them met weekly to pray, study the Scriptures and just talk about life in general. Rebecca was helping Tara establish her faith, and for the first time in Tara's life, it was becoming her own. Rebecca was incredibly encouraging, and she gave Tara insights as well as correction when necessary.

Tara discovered the freedom that comes from walking with Christ, and she wanted to share it with her friends. Rebecca continued to meet with her, and Tara began meeting with one of the younger girls, which helped her to move forward in her own faith.

The apostle Paul knew the people at the church of Thessalonica were struggling like Tara, so he sent Timothy to help establish them in their faith. Timothy lived with them, just did life with them, helped them know how to grow in their faith and encouraged them.

READ

1 THESSALONIANS 3:2

Focus on ...

"We sent Timothy, who is our brother and co-worker in God's service in spreading the gospel of Christ, to strengthen and encourage you in your faith ..." (v. 2).

DISCOVER

The basic truth is:

EXPERIENCE

As a result I will:

CONSIDER

- Do you have someone in your life who is mentoring you?
- All of us need someone as a mentor in our lives!
- Why would you not want a mentor involved in your life?
- What would it take for you to ask for help?

PRAY

In response to this passage, I will pray for:

JOURNAL

I just have to write about:

THINK

Mason wanted to begin an on-campus Bible study and prayer group at his public school, but he was uncertain about what to do. He remembered his youth pastor, Phil, had talked about this on several occasions, so he asked the pastor to meet with him. Mason had good intentions, but Phil also knew he tended to begin things and not finish them.

Before discussing the aspects of the campus meeting, Phil opened the Bible to Luke 14:27-32, and they read it together. Phil was very careful to ask questions, because he wanted Mason to be totally committed before beginning. He explained to Mason how he was taking up his cross and moving forward for God … and this did not include turning back.

Phil also talked to Mason about planning ahead. They discussed the time to meet, how to get the word out, how long to meet, who was going to speak, what materials to use and a dozen other details. Mason was a bit overwhelmed, but also thankful for the conversation.

Now Luke 14 is not just about planning details of a program: it is about being consistent with our faith. Our reputation is at stake, and it is a poor testimony for us to not have counted the cost up front.

READ

LUKE 14:27-32

Focus on ...
"And whoever does not carry their cross and follow me cannot be my disciple" (v 27).

DISCOVER

The basic truth is:

EXPERIENCE

As a result I will:

CONSIDER

- Our testimony and reputation are at stake when we fail to finish.
- True disciples count the cost and determine they will pay the price!
- Do you have a tendency to rush into things?
- Do you have someone in your life you can check in with as a mentor?

PRAY

In response to this passage, I will pray for:

_____

_____

_____

_____

JOURNAL

I just have to write about:

_____

_____

_____

_____

_____

_____

_____

_____

_____

_____

_____

_____

THINK

Olivia came to Christ at an evangelistic outreach event sponsored by the local church in her area. It was all new to her, as she was not from a Christian family and had no background in what it meant to live a godly life. Her only reference point was a grandmother who had died when she was only 6.

When one of the youth leaders named Rita reached out to her following the event, she was uncertain about how to respond. Rita seemed nice and sincerely concerned about her, but Olivia had been hurt by so many people that she was leery.

Rita's consistent kindness eventually won Olivia over, and they finally met for coffee at Starbucks. Olivia had never had anyone take a personal interest in her without having an agenda. It was apparent Rita had her best interest in mind and just wanted to help. Over the next few months they met for Bible study, Olivia spent time with Rita's family and Rita attended Olivia's school functions.

Olivia realized this was a person who loved God and loved people. She found herself wanting to be like Rita, even copying many of her habits. Olivia decided Rita set an example to follow and took advantage of the opportunity.

READ

PHILIPPIANS 3:17

Focus on...
"Join together in following my example, brothers and sisters, and just as you have us as a model, keep your eyes on those who live as we do" (v. 17).

DISCOVER

The basic truth is:

_____

_____

_____

_____

_____

EXPERIENCE

As a result I will:

_____

_____

_____

_____

_____

CONSIDER

- Everyone needs a godly example to follow.
- Do you know an adult whose pattern of life is worthy of following?
- Why do you think students are leery of allowing adults into their lives?
- Think about a person in your school who is like Olivia.

PRAY

In response to this passage, I will pray for:

JOURNAL

I just have to write about:

THINK

Micah held his breath as Mr. Hall tried to get the computer to work for his PowerPoint presentation. The lessons were great, but technology was not Mr. Hall's "thing." The truth was, he was terrible at it.

Micah had other suggestions for him, as well, suggestions about how he could use social media to promote events. Every time Mr. Hall handed out another piece of paper with a prayer request on it, he thought about the tree that had been killed and how most of the papers were going to be thrown away. He had a better idea, but he was just a student.

As he sat there, 1 Timothy 4:12 came to his mind. The pastor had just spoken on the verse a couple of weeks earlier. Micah was much younger than Mr. Hall, but his motives were pure: a desire for ministry excellence. He also knew that more students could be reached through more effective communication.

He approached Mr. Hall with his ideas and was pleasantly surprised to find he was open to everything. Mr. Hall wanted to reach more students as well, but he needed help. Micah teamed up with him for a little "reverse mentoring," and the two of them began to see the ministry grow.

READ

1 TIMOTHY 4:12-16

Focus on ...

"Don't let anyone look down on you because you are young, but set an example for the believers in speech, in conduct, in love, in faith and in purity" (v. 12).

DISCOVER

The basic truth is:

EXPERIENCE

As a result I will:

CONSIDER

- Some of the best ministries use people of various ages in leadership.
- Maybe an adult is just waiting on a student to step up.
- Are you willing to do a little "reverse mentoring"?
- What could you offer to the youth ministry to increase its effectiveness?

PRAY

In response to this passage, I will pray for:

JOURNAL

I just have to write about:

THINK

Have you ever been truly motivated by a special speaker and what he/she had to share? Some people are challenging speakers, but some speakers deliver *timeless* messages. Timeless speeches are as motivating today as they were when originally delivered—speeches such as Abraham Lincoln's *Gettysburg Address* or Martin Luther King's *I Have a Dream speech*.

One such speech was delivered by Winston Churchill, prime minister of England, when he returned to speak at Harrow School. By the way, that is the same school from which he almost flunked out years before. At the time of the speech, the war upon England was facing some desperate days.

It was October 29, 1941 when he took time to speak to the students. His speech was two pages long, but 29 words took on a life of their own. These words have been quoted thousands of times.

Churchill said, " ... *never give in, never give in, never, never, never, never-in nothing, great or small, large or petty—never give in except to convictions of honor and good sense.*" It is easy to see why these words have become immortal, isn't it?

In our passage today, the apostles' words motivated the people, as well. They had come to give instruction and to strengthen the people. One of the great roles of a mentor is to inspire or motivate others with their life and words.

READ

ACTS 15:30-35

Focus on ...

"Judas and Silas, who themselves were prophets, said much to encourage and strengthen the believers" (v. 32).

DISCOVER

The basic truth is:

EXPERIENCE

As a result I will:

CONSIDER

- One of the roles of a mentor is to motivate others.
- A mentor's words are only as motivating as his life.
- Who motivates you?
- Think about a speech you have heard that motivated you.

PRAY

In response to this passage, I will pray for:

JOURNAL

I just have to write about:

THINK

The American bald eagle is a majestic bird. Just the sight of one soaring overhead is cause to pause. While they were moved from the endangered species list to the threatened species list in 1995, their future is still questionable.

Eagles are amazing birds with incredible capabilities. Their keen eyesight allows them to spot a fish from up to a mile away, giving them an unfair advantage over their prey. Unlike the human eye that can distinguish three colors, they have the ability to distinguish five.

The seven-foot wing span and small body allows them to fly at speeds of up to 35 mph and dive from the sky at up to 100 mph. Plus they can effortlessly soar on the currents for hours and climb to heights of 10,000 feet.

No wonder God chose this remarkable creature for the illustration in Isaiah 4o:31. What a great encouragement to think we could soar on the heights, have this kind of strength and access abilities beyond what we possess within ourselves.

The passage you are reading today is extremely encouraging. The prophet Isaiah reminds us we are not in this alone! We can gain strength from God above.

READ

ISAIAH 40:28-31

Focus on ...
" ... but those who hope in the Lord
will renew their strength.
They will soar on wings like eagles;
they will run and not grow weary,
they will walk and not be faint" (v. 31).

DISCOVER

The basic truth is:

EXPERIENCE

As a result I will:

CONSIDER

- The eagle channels its power into effortless soaring in the heights.
- Eagles are selective about relationships—they don't hang with turkeys.
- Can you picture yourself resting in the fact that God has your back?
- What lessons can you learn from the eagle?

PRAY

In response to this passage, I will pray for:

JOURNAL

I just have to write about:

THINK

The world of bullying is not a new concept. It has been around as long as mankind. Perhaps today it is more pronounced because we have added the cyberbullying aspect to it. Once it took place only in public, but now it can happen in private—and even come right into your bedroom!

Throughout history there have been those who have stood up against the bullies on behalf of those who could not stand up for themselves. Others took the risk to become the "voice of the voiceless," speaking up for those who could not speak for themselves. People like:

- Helen Keller (1880-1968): Deaf and blind from early childhood, she overcame her disability to tirelessly campaign on behalf of deaf and blind people.
- Frederick Douglass (1818-1895): A former slave who was committed to working for the emancipation of all slaves and ending the injustice of slavery and racism in America.
- Dietrich Bonhoeffer (1906-1945): A principled Christian activist who opposed the Nazi regime in Germany and was killed for it.
- Malala Yousafzai (1997-): A Pakistani schoolgirl who defied threats from the Taliban to campaign for Pakistani girls' right to education. She survived being shot in the head by the Taliban and has become a global advocate for human, women and educational rights.

Taking a stand for things that are right is a risk. Becoming a "voice for the voiceless" is often costly, but honorable. Our passage today challenges us to speak up but also to work for those in need. Go ahead! Take the risk ... be **ONE**!

READ

PROVERBS 31:8-9

Focus on ...
"Speak up for those who cannot speak for themselves,
for the rights of all who are destitute.
Speak up and judge fairly;
defend the rights of the poor and needy" (v. 8-9).

DISCOVER

The basic truth is:

EXPERIENCE

As a result I will:

CONSIDER

- Being a voice for the voiceless is not only right, it is biblical!
- Bullies count on the fact that no one will say anything.
- Are you willing to be the **ONE** who stands up and speaks up?
- Think about a situation where you can be that **ONE**.

PRAY

In response to this passage, I will pray for:

JOURNAL

I just have to write about:

THINK

The story in the book of Philemon is one of those stories you do not want to miss. It is short: the entire book is just 25 verses long. If you are not careful, you can miss it when you turn from Titus to Hebrews in the New Testament.

Here is the synopsis of the book. Onesimus is a runaway slave. He has run away from his master, Philemon, who is a believer. He reaches Rome where he meets the Apostle Paul in jail, and Paul leads him to faith in Christ. (Wow!)

Now Paul writes this little letter to Philemon to tell him that Onesimus is coming back home. By Roman law he is supposed to be put to death for running away, but Paul says, "You need to receive him as a brother in Christ." He goes on to say, "Remember Philemon, I led you to Christ, and I want you to do everything for Onesimus you would do for me. " (Wow again!)

Paul basically says, "This man is my friend and my brother. He has been a great help to me, and I would really like to have him stay with me." Think about it. According to the world's system, this is a lowly runaway slave under the penalty of death. But here he is—hanging out with the best Christian on the planet.

Paul had no concern for class structures. To him there were only two classes of people—lost or saved. We need to follow Paul's example and begin some peacemaking in the world where we live every day.

READ

Focus on ...

" ... that I appeal to you for my son Onesimus, who became my son while I was in chains. Formerly he was useless to you, but now he has become useful both to you and to me" (vv. 10-11).

DISCOVER

The basic truth is:

EXPERIENCE

As a result I will:

CONSIDER

- The apostle Paul did not care where you came from but about where you were going.
- Paul proved his commitment to Onesimus by writing to Philemon on his behalf.
- Do you know someone like Philemon who needs your friendship?
- What would reconciliation look like at your school?

PRAY

In response to this passage, I will pray for:

_____

_____

_____

_____

JOURNAL

I just have to write about:

_____

_____

_____

_____

_____

_____

THINK

Emma noticed Adeelah the first day of school. The entire first week, she felt she should welcome Adeelah to the school, but she did not know what to say. After all, she had never actually had a conversation with a Muslim before.

Unfortunately, everyone else was doing the same thing, and Adeelah felt alone. After a couple of weeks, it became a joke to some of the students, and they began to dare each other to see who would be the first person to talk to the "terrorist."

Adeelah heard the laughter behind her back and even caught wind of the joke about being a "terrorist," and it hurt her deeply. She was Muslim, but her family had come to the United States to flee a dictator and persecution. She longed to know someone, but no one even engaged her in conversation.

Emma finally had enough, and her Christian conviction wouldn't allow her to stand idly by any longer. At lunch one day, Emma approached Adeelah at the table where she always sat alone and asked if she could join her. They both could hear the snickers of the other students, but Emma did not care, and Adeelah was just happy to have a friend.

Over the next few weeks they developed a relationship, and eventually a couple of other Christian students joined them. One day, Adeelah asked Emma a very pointed question: "Why did you reach out to me when no one else seemed to care?"

Emma smiled, knowing God was opening the door for her to share about her Savior. Just like Jesus did in our passage today, Emma crossed cultural lines, which gave her the opportunity to share about the Living Water.

READ

JOHN 4:7-26

Focus on ...

"The Samaritan woman said to him, 'You are a Jew and I am a Samaritan woman. How can you ask me for a drink?' (For Jews do not associate with Samaritans)" (v. 9).

DISCOVER

The basic truth is:

EXPERIENCE

As a result I will:

CONSIDER

- Jesus crossed the cultural lines because it was right, and it opened doors for the gospel.
- Being nice to people should not be based on the expectation that they are going to listen to the gospel.
- Are you willing to cross cultural lines to demonstrate Christ's love?
- Why do you think people make fun of those who are different?

PRAY

In response to this passage, I will pray for:

JOURNAL

I just have to write about:

THINK

It happened again. Ralph and the youth leaders had worked hard to bring visitors to the youth group, and the guests were being ignored. Even if they had been welcomed into the group, who would want to be part of this group?

The students didn't get along with each other, they were constantly putting each other down and no one was showing love. This is not the type of group you would want to join if you were looking for fellowship or just a "safe place" to hang out.

Ralph decided this had to be addressed with the youth group, but he knew preaching at them was not the answer. The next time they met, he read John 13:31-35 and then put verses 34-35 on the screen. He paused for a moment before going into a series of questions.

- If you were not a Christian, would this group make you want to become one?
- If you did not know anyone in this group and you just showed up needing help, do you think you could find it here?
- Why do we act the way we do, as shown in this group?
- Did Jesus give us a suggestion or commandment about loving others?
- If people know we are His disciples by our love, then who do *outsiders* think we *are*, based on our actions last week?

Ralph's actions led to some great discussion. Some of the students even shared how they did not realize the way they were acting and actually asked for forgiveness. It was the beginning of a change. Ralph hoped it would be a change that resulted in a significant impact!

READ

JOHN 13:31-35

Focus on ...

"A new command I give you: Love one another. As I have loved you, so you must love one another. By this everyone will know that you are my disciples, if you love one another" (vv. 34-35).

DISCOVER

The basic truth is:

EXPERIENCE

As a result I will:

CONSIDER

- True disciples of Jesus are known by their love for one another.
- Jesus gave us a command—not a suggestion—to *love one another*.
- Do visitors feel safe in your youth group?
- Do people know you are a disciple of Jesus by your love?

PRAY

In response to this passage, I will pray for:

JOURNAL

I just have to write about:

THINK

The strength of the body of Christ is that every believer is different. We all have different gifts and abilities. Some speak, some sing and others work with their hands. Regardless of what you do, your ability is your **platform** for sharing the gospel.

Telling people about Jesus is not just for preachers and evangelists—it is for every believer. It does not matter who you are and what your gift is. You can be a witness for Jesus. In fact, there are some people who will listen to *you* but will never listen to your preacher.

They will listen to you because they respect you for your particular gift or ability. That is why I say it is your **platform**! Whatever causes people to stop and listen to the gospel is the **platform** God has given you, so don't waste it.

Maybe you have an outgoing personality or maybe you are quiet and reserved. It does not matter—God can use you.

The passage for today reminds us that God gave us our **platform** so we can serve and reach others with the gospel. The apostle Peter challenges us to be good stewards of those gifts because they were given by the grace of God. So stand on your **platform**, and use your gift today!

READ

1 PETER 4:7-11

Focus on ...

"Each of you should use whatever gift you have received to serve others, as faithful stewards of God's grace in its various forms. If anyone speaks, they should do so as one who speaks the very words of God. If anyone serves, they should do so with the strength God provides, so that in all things God may be praised through Jesus Christ. To him be the glory and the power for ever and ever. Amen" (vv. 10-11).

DISCOVER

The basic truth is:

_____

_____

_____

_____

EXPERIENCE

As a result I will:

_____

_____

_____

_____

CONSIDER

- Every **platform** is a launching pad for the gospel!
- God gives us our **platform** gifts so we can serve.
- Do you know what your **platform** gift is?
- Talk to a trusted adult about what your **platform** gift is so you can begin using if for God.

PRAY

In response to this passage, I will pray for:

JOURNAL

I just have to write about:

THINK

Ava (not her real name) was a normal 13-year-old girl. She loved music and movies and dreamed of becoming a writer one day. She was plain in appearance, and because her family struggled financially, her clothes were not designer like most of the other students at school.

At home Ava was either ignored or treated like a servant. She basically had missed her childhood because of some pressures in the home with her mom and dad. School was even worse, as she was bullied and ridiculed day after day.

Ava was teased about the way she dressed, talked, ate and anything else her peers could find to use against her. She just wanted one person to take up for her or be a friend, but it never happened.

Night after night, she wrote about the pain in her journal as she cried. She even put a couple of thoughts on Facebook, hoping someone would see her desperation and reach out. She had to do something: she could not continue like this.

So, on a Monday morning in October, she got up, changed the status of her Facebook page to indicate that she was going to kill herself and walked out the door. She had lost hope!

People can live without many things, but they cannot live without hope. There are thousands of Avas all across this globe who need to experience the hope that can only come through Jesus. This is a gift that you and I can keep giving away as we share Jesus and His love with others.

READ

1 PETER 1:3-9

Focus on ...

"Praise be to the God and Father of our Lord Jesus Christ! In his great mercy he has given us new birth into a living hope through the resurrection of Jesus Christ from the dead ..." (v. 3).

DISCOVER

The basic truth is:

EXPERIENCE

As a result I will:

CONSIDER

- God wants us to experience hope through His Son Jesus.
- Our hope is living because Jesus came back from the dead.
- People can live without many things, but not without hope.
- Are you willing to help people experience hope through Jesus?

PRAY

In response to this passage, I will pray for:

_____

_____

_____

_____

_____

JOURNAL

I just have to write about:

_____

_____

_____

_____

_____

_____

_____

THINK

The following story was told about a Korean mother during the Korean Conflict … A pregnant woman was caught in a snow storm as she tried to reach safety so she could deliver her baby out of the war zone. She pushed through the elements, headed for a warm house and good friends.

Suddenly she was overtaken with labor pains. She tried to keep moving, as she feared having the baby alone in the storm. However, the pains became stronger, and she had no choice.

She found shelter under a bridge and some reprieve from the falling snow. It was a less than desirable site, but there she gave birth to a baby boy. Now she had another dilemma: she had no clothing for the baby.

The only thing she could do was take off some of her own clothing and wrap it around the baby. Then she gently cuddled up to the child so her body heat would keep him warm.

The next morning, her friends—who had been out searching for her during the night—came to the bridge and heard the muffled cries of the baby. The mother had frozen to death from exposure but the baby boy was alive.

Years later the boy requested to go back to the bridge. As he stood there with the friends, who had adopted him, he asked them for a favor. He said, "Tell me again what my mother did for me the night she died so I could live!"

The story may be folklore or true. Either way it drives home the point. It is a great reminder that helps us *realize* what Jesus did when He died so we could live!

READ

Focus on ...

"But God demonstrates his own love for us in this: While we were still sinners, Christ died for us" (v. 8).

DISCOVER

The basic truth is:

_____

_____

_____

_____

EXPERIENCE

As a result I will:

_____

_____

_____

_____

_____

CONSIDER

- Jesus sacrificed His life for us so we could live.
- Jesus proved His love for us when He died for us while we were still sinners.
- We must come to the place where we *realize* what Jesus did for us and that we need a Savior.
- When did you *realize* Jesus was God's Son and you needed him and his salvation?

PRAY

In response to this passage, I will pray for:

JOURNAL

I just have to write about:

THINK

Let's talk about broken relationships. Obviously, it depends on the level of the relationship, but if a deep relationship is severed, the effects are magnified. Probably all of us have dealt with this at some point. Honestly answer the follow survey, based on your experience.

When I was dealing with a broken relationship, I experienced the following:
(Put a check mark in the box of each that applies.)

Anger	Depression
Pain	Anxiety
Guilt	Hopelessness
Fear	Thoughts of revenge
Insecurity	Apathy
Ineffectiveness	Loneliness

When a human relationship is broken or is suffering, we can be part of the solution. Apologizing or taking the necessary steps to repair damaged feelings or connections go a long way. However, when it comes to our broken relationship with God, it is different. Only God Himself, through His Son Jesus, can **restore** that relationship.

Our relationship was broken by our sin, but Jesus the sinless One came to Earth to take care of our sin problem. He lived a sinless, spotless life; died on the cross, was buried and rose again to **restore** our relationship. He offers this to us as a free gift, but we must respond and *take* it. This is great news for us and for the whole world!

READ

1 CORINTHIANS 15:1-8

Focus on ...

"For what I received I passed on to you as of first importance: that Christ died for our sins according to the Scriptures, that he was buried, that he was raised on the third day according to the Scriptures..." (vv. 3-4).

DISCOVER

The basic truth is:

EXPERIENCE

As a result I will:

CONSIDER

- Broken relationships are stressful and can be consuming.
- Our relationship with God was broken by our sin.
- Jesus **restored** our relations by His death, burial and resurrection.
- With whom have you shared the message of how to have a **restored** relationship with God?

PRAY

In response to this passage, I will pray for:

JOURNAL

I just have to write about:

DAY 25

THINK

Do you like to attend weddings, or are they simply torture for you? Most students either love them or endure them, but few are neutral.

Regardless of your feelings, let's talk about the ceremonial aspect of all weddings. Every wedding is different. Some cost thousands of dollars and others cost very little. Some are fashionably decorated, others are plain. Some last for hours, and some are short, sweet and to the point.

Whether you pay $100 or $10,000 for the wedding, one component is part of all weddings: the vows. Not all vows are identical, but basically they all come to the point of saying, "I do." These two little words are words of acceptance and commitment.

In a similar way, a person has to express to Jesus his or her acceptance of Christ's free gift of salvation. We must **realize** we are sinners for whom Jesus died and acknowledge He has **restored** our broken relationship by His death, burial and resurrection. Then we need to say "YES" and **receive** His free gift of salvation.

READ

ROMANS 10:9-13

Focus on ...
" ... for, 'Everyone who calls on the name of the Lord will be saved'" (v. 13).

DISCOVER

The basic truth is:

_____

_____

_____

_____

EXPERIENCE

As a result I will:

_____

_____

_____

_____

_____

_____

CONSIDER

- Anyone who calls on Jesus can be saved, according to Romans 10:13.
- Saying "YES" to Jesus' free gift of salvation is like the "I do" in a wedding.
- Have you ever shared your faith with anyone else?
- Identify one person you intend to talk to about Jesus this week:

_____

PRAY

In response to this passage, I will pray for:

JOURNAL

I just have to write about:

THINK

The Two Line Wire Bridge in a high ropes course is a half-inch thick and 40 feet off the ground. The thought of stepping out onto the wire can simultaneously bring feelings of anticipation and fear.

Likewise, helping someone grow in their newly found faith can be a little scary, but it also can be one of the greatest adventures of your life. You can *"influence"* the direction of the rest of their life by jump-starting them at the beginning.

In the New Testament book of Colossians, we find a challenge for believers beginning their new adventure in faith. This outline can serve as an outline for the process. In Colossians 2:6-7, the apostle Paul condenses the Christian life down to three basic stages:

Know
"As you therefore have received Christ Jesus the Lord ..."

Grow
"... so walk in Him, rooted and built up in Him and established in the faith, as you have been taught ..."

Show
"... as you have been taught, abounding in it with thanksgiving."

READ

COLOSSIANS 2:6-10

Focus on...

"So then, just as you received Christ Jesus as Lord, continue to live your lives in him, rooted and built up in him, strengthened in the faith as you were taught, and overflowing with thankfulness" (vv. 6-7).

DISCOVER

The basic truth is:

EXPERIENCE

As a result I will:

CONSIDER

- Saying "YES" to Jesus is the beginning of a great adventure!
- Once we say "YES" to Jesus, we need to be rooted in our faith.
- If we are to "walk worthy" of the Lord, we must know what pleases Him.
- Are you ready to "influence" people for Christ?

PRAY

In response to this passage, I will pray for:

_____

_____

_____

_____

JOURNAL

I just have to write about:

_____

_____

_____

_____

_____

_____

_____

THINK

If you wanted to be a great basketball player, would you ask a hockey player to teach you? If you wanted to be an accomplished pianist, would you solicit a carpenter to be your tutor?

When you set your sights on becoming proficient in a particular area of life, you usually look for experienced teachers who can push your skills and develop your abilities. The same is true in the Christian life, especially in the early days of your faith.

Do *you* have a spiritual coach who can give you guidance? Do you know what it takes to be someone's spiritual coach? A good coach is someone who can give you encouragement and support through accountability. Here is what to look for in a spiritual coach:

- Someone whose life is worthy of imitation—1 Corinthians 11:1—"*Follow my example, as I follow the example of Christ.*"
- Someone who has proven himself/herself in a particular field of interest. The coach is not perfect but has had a measure of success qualifying him or her to lead.
- Someone older who has walked with Christ and demonstrated a faithful lifestyle before others— 1 Peter 5:5—"*In the same way, you who are younger, submit yourselves to your elders.*"
- Someone like a spiritual father or mother caring for you as a new "baby" in Christ—1 Thessalonians 2:11—"*For you know that we dealt with each of you as a father deals with his own children ...*"

Maybe you'd like to serve as a spiritual coach–and maybe you feel like you *need* one. If so, talk to a parent, pastor or trusted leader and ask them to help. If you think you would like to serve in this area, *go for it*!

READ

1 PETER 5:1-5

Focus on...
"In the same way, you who are younger, submit yourselves to your elders. All of you, clothe yourselves with humility toward one another, because, 'God opposes the proud but shows favor to the humble'" (v. 5)

DISCOVER

The basic truth is:

_____

_____

_____

_____

EXPERIENCE

As a result I will:

_____

_____

_____

_____

_____

CONSIDER

- Spiritual coaches are not perfect, they just have a track record.
- A spiritual coach's life should be worthy of imitation!
- Did anyone ever coach you in your faith?
- Would you like a spiritual coach to help you move forward in your faith?

PRAY

In response to this passage, I will pray for:

JOURNAL

I just have to write about:

THINK

Jacob and Noah began their friendship in grammar school. During their freshman year of high school, they started competing at almost everything. They even found a way to make boring activities a competition.

They went to youth group together at the same church and had the same leader, Brian. Brian was amused at the way the pair competed, but he also knew they had a deep friendship and the competition was all done in fun.

Brian decided to help the two guys use their competitive spirit for a good purpose. He spoke to them about being spiritual accountability partners. He explained they both needed to grow in their faith and encouraged them to push one another forward spiritually.

At first they joked about who would be the "Best Christian," but it wasn't long before they were both maturing in their faith. As they pushed each other along in spiritual disciplines, both realized the benefits of having a friend at the peer level who cared about his spiritual condition.

You need to lock arms with other Christians who are practicing their faith. Find a friend who loves the Lord and who can help you on your journey. As our passage for today says, there are going to be times when you stumble and need someone to help you up.

READ

ECCLESIASTES 4:9-12

Focus on ...
"Two are better than one,
because they have a good return for their labor:
If either of them falls down,
one can help the other up.
But pity anyone who falls
and has no one to help them up" (vv. 9-10).

DISCOVER

The basic truth is:

EXPERIENCE

As a result I will:

CONSIDER

- Brian decided to turn Jacob and Noah's competition into something to benefit their faith.
- Peer accountability relationships are vital to a student's life.
- When have you needed a friend to hold you spiritually accountable?
- What are a couple of benefits of peer accountability, according to our passage today?

PRAY

In response to this passage, I will pray for:

JOURNAL

I just have to write about:

THINK

Picture yourself in the following scene:

You are a soldier deep in enemy territory. As the morning dawns, you roll out of your bunk and hurriedly dress for the day's activities. Quickly you contemplate all the things you intend to accomplish during the day.

Anticipation turns to activity as you walk out into the blazing desert sun. Without any hesitation, you pick up your weapon and head off toward enemy lines, never once checking the orders of the day or communicating with the Commander in Chief. After all, you are in a hurry, and there are so many things to be done.

No soldier in his right mind would ever be so foolish, yet Christian students (and adults) like yourself follow such a scenario every day as they go out into the world. The enemy they face is much more cunning and deadly than any human dictator this world knows. He takes prisoners at will and is capable of defeating even the most formidable foe.

Every student needs to develop the godly habit of meeting the Commander in Chief each day. There is no substitute for meeting with God every morning to prepare for the battle. Before you hurry out into "no man's land," learn to practice the art of quiet time.

Quiet time is more than just sitting quietly in a place of solitude: it's a divine appointment. It is an opportunity to pray, read God's Word and prepare one's heart for the pressures, trials and opportunities of the coming day.

READ

PSALM 143:1-12

Focus on ...
"Let the morning bring me word of your unfailing love,
for I have put my trust in you.
Show me the way I should go,
for to you I entrust my life" (v. 8).

DISCOVER

The basic truth is:

EXPERIENCE

As a result I will:

CONSIDER

- Devotional time with God is vital to our spiritual health.
- When we meet alone with God, we are developing a relationship.
- Do you know how to have a quiet time with God?
- Meet with someone you respect and ask questions about making your devotional time with God more effective.

PRAY

In response to this passage, I will pray for:

JOURNAL

I just have to write about:

THINK

It is amusing to watch children play a game of tag! They run after each other, desperately trying to tag the next person. One of them yells, "You can't touch me! I am in the safe place!"

We all need to know we have a safe place. Your local church should be your safe place. It is not a place to hide from the realities of the world, but rather a place to learn how to face them. It can be a place of learning and growing, a place of support and encouragement.

If you have said "yes" to Jesus' free gift of salvation, you have become God's child. You also became part of a big family. You have all kinds of new relatives who want to love and care for you at your church. You will make new friends your age and older. These people will pray for you, love you and give you guidance. They will help you on your faith journey.

Remember, church is not only about what you *get*; it is a place for you to *serve* the Lord. You will want to make a commitment to be faithful and to help others. As a part of the family, everyone has a responsibility to encourage one another and be involved.

READ

HEBREWS 10:19-25

Focus on...
"Not giving up meeting together, as some are in the habit of doing, but encouraging one another—and all the more as you see the Day approaching" (v. 25).

DISCOVER

The basic truth is:

EXPERIENCE

As a result I will:

CONSIDER

- In an unsafe world, everyone needs a "safe place."
- The local church is the "safe place" for many people.
- Are you connecting with your Christian family at the "safe place"?
- Do you serve and give back to the Christian family at the "safe place"?

PRAY

In response to this passage, I will pray for:

_____

_____

_____

_____

JOURNAL

I just have to write about:

_____

_____

_____

_____

_____

_____

_____

_____

_____

_____

_____

_____

NOTES